Table of Contents

DEDICATION 2
INTRODUCTION 3
PART 1 7
   Before You Start Recruiting Affiliates 7
PART 2 10
   Recruiting Affiliates 10
PART 3 27
   Educating Affiliates 27
PART 4 32
   Retaining Affiliates 32

DEDICATION

For all of the affiliate managers out there. It's so much more than a job – it's a balancing act built on passion. Thank you for all you do.

INTRODUCTION

The management of affiliate programs has changed over the years. I got my first affiliate management job in 1997, and I didn't have any experience at the time.

To say I bluffed my way into the job would be an understatement. At the time, I didn't have any experience in, or knowledge of, marketing. Not a single class in college. Nothing. My sole strength for the position was that I recently had become an affiliate at Amazon, so I could talk the talk.

Fortunately, the company that was hiring was focused on creating an online medical bookstore in the model of Amazon.

And I was willing to work for cheap.

So, I got the job. That was the easy part. Then I actually had to figure out how to start and manage an affiliate program.

Making It Up

Back in the 1990's there were no resources for affiliate marketers. None that I could find, anyway. I couldn't even locate another affiliate manager in all of New York City. So I had to create processes to build the affiliate program.

It was a challenge to recruit affiliates at that time because no one had heard of affiliate marketing. I decided that the way to go was to drop the word "affiliate" and focus on the opportunity to earn money by merchandising the company's existing website.

In my view, everyone I brought on was a salesperson for the company, and they should be treated as such. That led me to devise an educational program for the new affiliates, as well as ways to retain them after they joined.

My three-pronged approach to affiliate relationships (recruit, educate, retain) resulted in a high percentage of active affiliates. At the time, I was disappointed with having "only" half of my affiliates putting up links and nearly all of them producing sales.

But I later learned that it was typical for an affiliate program to follow the Pareto principle, also known as the 80/20 rule, where 80% of affiliate activity is generated by 20% of affiliates. That was the standard I started hearing anyway. It turned out that 98/2 was more like it for many affiliate programs.

Quality vs. Quantity

One of the reasons for such unbalanced affiliate programs was the misguided view that more is better.

This was symbolized in the keynote address at the Affiliate Solutions NYC conference in December 1999. The then President/CEO of FreeShop, Tim Choate, caused jaws to drop when he revealed a big milestone for his company.

They had reached 100,000 affiliates in their affiliate program. Not 100,000 who had gotten a check or even put up a link. They just had 100,000 on the books.

Talk about false pride and misguided metrics. The crowd was in awe of this sexy six-figure number of affiliates. No one asked about the percentage of active affiliates or whether the company was concerned about having legions of un-checked affiliates represent the brand.

This was before the dot-com bubble burst, and bigger was better. Quantity *was* quality in those irrational days for most affiliate marketers.

End of an Error

The idea that having a massive number of affiliates was an indicator of a prosperous affiliate program took a hit in the spring of 2001.

It was all because of a guy named Mark McElwain who created a site featuring a series of messages left on his answering machine by his "psycho" ex-girlfriend. The site also featured a bunch of affiliate program banners.

This wasn't a problem until there was an article in *The Wall Street Journal* that mentioned how the site was "sponsored" by advertisers including Moviefone.com and *Sports Illustrated*.

All of the affiliate programs with banners on PsychoExGirlfriend.com claimed ignorance of their association with the site and promptly blamed the affiliate marketing channel.

Well, it's true that they were ignorant, but this mess was of their own making, as they wanted to get big and do so fast.

Accountability was for suckers when there was a convenient scapegoat. The whole story became an indictment of affiliate marketing and the lack of oversight. Suddenly, affiliate managers shifted from automatic to manual approval for affiliate applications.

The funny thing was that the option to approve affiliates manually was always there. But, prior to some companies having an embarrassing association with an affiliate, automatic approval was the method of choice, since volumes of affiliates brought smiles to the faces of venture capitalists and CEOs.

Now What?

All of this leads to one important thing to understand, which is that affiliate marketing is all about relationships.

You want to have affiliates you can trust representing your brand. That means you should know each affiliate in your affiliate program and have an ongoing dialogue with them.

Sure, you'll get some affiliates who apply to your affiliate program organically through exposure in an affiliate network, but it is your responsibility to actively recruit the affiliates you think will be the best fit for your company.

And, just like I was doing way back when, you should treat them like your sales team. That means you provide them with the educational materials they need to best promote you; and you also focus on retaining them, because it's a whole lot easier to keep the affiliates you have than it is to replace them.

You should be recruiting all the time so that your base of quality affiliates continues to grow.

Please read through my tactics that follow, but don't stop there. Apply them, too.

PART 1

Before You Start Recruiting Affiliates

"I didn't invent the rainy day, man. I just own the best umbrella." - Dennis Hope (Almost Famous)

The movie *Field of Dreams* popularized the phrase "If you build it, they will come." That might apply to clearing out a corn field to build a baseball diamond, but it's not the case with affiliate programs.

In addition to putting together a fantastic affiliate program, you need to become the biggest cheerleader, evangelist, marketing wiz, and recruiter for your affiliate program in order to get the attention of quality, relevant affiliates.

First things first, though. You need to create the best affiliate program in your vertical. Affiliate Program Optimization (APO) is essential if you want to have an attractive affiliate program to promote to affiliates.

What Do Affiliates Look for in Affiliate Programs?

In the 2013 Affiliate Summit AffStat Report, affiliates were asked "When selecting a merchant to promote, what are the top three factors that sway your decision?"

Commission was most important, followed by product or service relevancy, affiliate network or tracking platform, brand awareness, and merchant reputation.

Here are the complete results from that question:

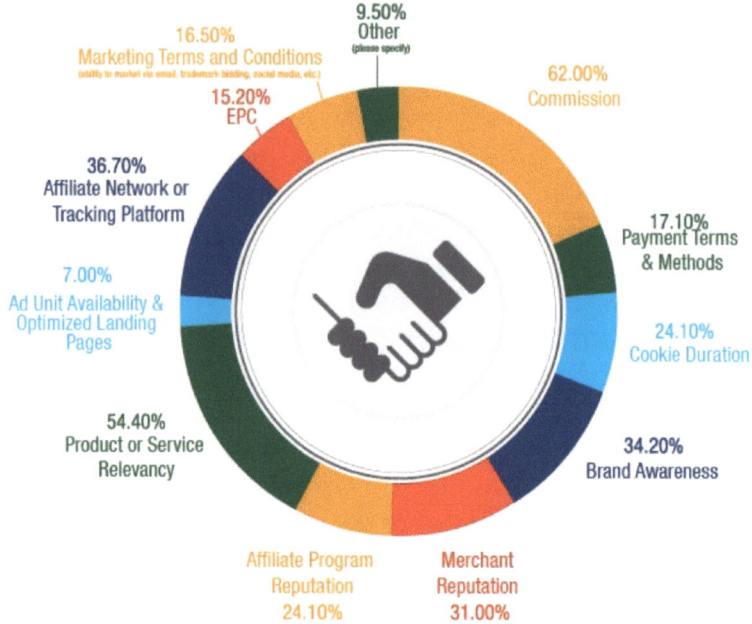

More than 1,600 affiliates were surveyed on their methods, preferences, and strategies for the 2013 Affiliate Summit AffStat Report.

You can find all sorts of other free data on affiliates at AffStat.com.

What is Affiliate Program Optimization?

APO is the process of going through the elements of your affiliate program to ensure that they are as good as or better than those of your direct competition.

Areas to look over and compare to your competitors include the method of affiliate approval (it should be manual), cookie length (better than the other companies in your space), and your commission rate (best in your vertical, within reason).

Also, look up the latest IAB (Internet Advertising Bureau) ad standards and creative guidelines, and make the standard banner sizes are available.

Then there is the EPC (average earnings per click), and you should know this, so you can share it with prospective affiliates. Often, you can see the numbers for your competitors in their respective affiliate networks.

If your EPC stinks by comparison, it is time to analyze why the conversion ratios are lousy and address the reasons.

How about your payment terms? Are they in line with other companies you are battling for affiliate attention?

Your TOS (terms of service)/affiliate agreement should be more than some boilerplate legalese. Be sure it includes any prohibited activity, such as bidding in paid search, using trademarks, promoting on coupon sites, etc.

You should have a guide for new affiliates to read through – a sort of new employee manual. This also goes for an affiliate resource site. I will detail these later in this book.

Finally, you must have a direct contact name publicly available and in any email correspondence. Also, it's a plus if you give affiliates the option to reach you via Facebook, LinkedIn, Twitter, etc.

PART 2

Recruiting Affiliates

"Hire people who are better than you are, then leave them to get on with it. Look for people who will aim for the remarkable, who will not settle for the routine." - David Ogilvy

Let me get this out of the way at the start – an affiliate program is not a media buy. You can't set it and forget it. An affiliate program requires ongoing management.

A core activity in a successful affiliate program is recruiting.

Some affiliates will apply to your program on their own, but that simply is not enough to sustain and grow an affiliate program. The people who come upon your application will be limited in number, and they won't necessarily be relevant.

So it's key to focus on proactively recruiting affiliates in a variety of areas after you have optimized your affiliate program.

But don't be tempted to go with a shotgun approach. You should have a reason for wanting to recruit each new affiliate.

Since you are pursuing these affiliates, I'd also recommend offering a higher commission rate to them as an incentive. But make it available for a limited time only to try and get them to join sooner rather than later.

I'll share the methods I've used over the years to effectively recruit quality affiliates for programs ranging from tiny Mom and Pops to Fortune 500 companies.

How Affiliates Find Affiliate Programs

When you are trying to recruit affiliates, it's important to know where they are looking for affiliate programs so you are there with information about your affiliate program.

In the 2013 Affiliate Summit AffStat Report, affiliates were asked "How do you typically find out about new affiliate programs? Select all that apply."

Affiliate information on the merchant website was the most frequent response, followed by the affiliate manager reaching out to them directly, affiliate or CPA network sites, and searches on Google, Yahoo, etc.

My guess as to why so many affiliates are finding out about new affiliate programs on the company sites is that some are arriving there due to various marketing efforts.

Here are the complete results from that question:

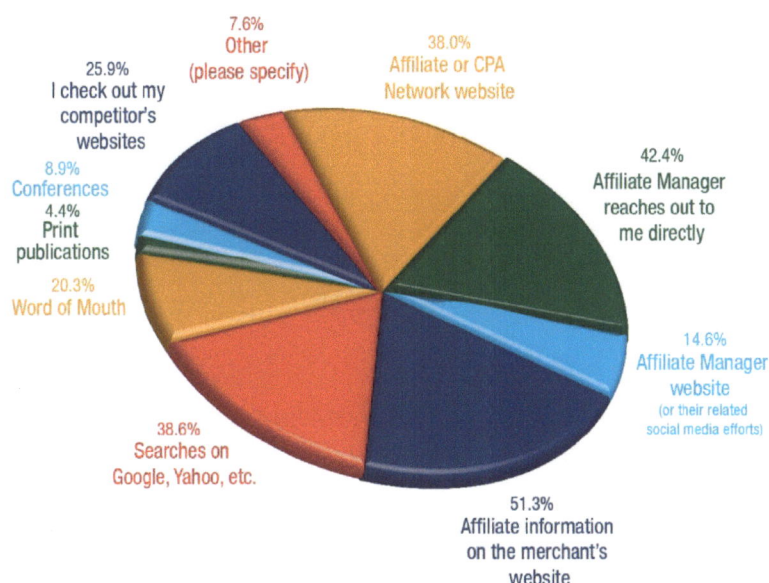

I think all of these responses, aside from the one about finding information on the merchant's site, deserve more attention, so I will break them down:

Affiliate Manager Reaches Out to Me Directly

This response covers reaching out to affiliates by way of email, IM, or phone. In my experience, email has been far easier to find than IM or phone, and affiliates have been more receptive to initial contacts by email.

I generally used email to set up a future conversation by IM or phone.

The initial email would be brief and it would highlight the main value propositions of the affiliate program, as well as provide my contact information and a link to join the affiliate program.

Note that I said join and not apply. Be sure to keep a list of people you have invited to join and then automatically accept them when you see their application come through.

I've goofed and rejected people I had invited to my affiliate programs in the past, but they usually were good natured after I apologized.

Searches on Google, Yahoo, etc.

Affiliates that want to promote your company often will look for your company name and the words "affiliate program" in search engines.

Be sure to make this search as easy as possible for them by having the page on your company site titled "Company Name Affiliate Program."

Dell does a good job with this and they repeat those keywords a number of times to optimize their page for the search engines.

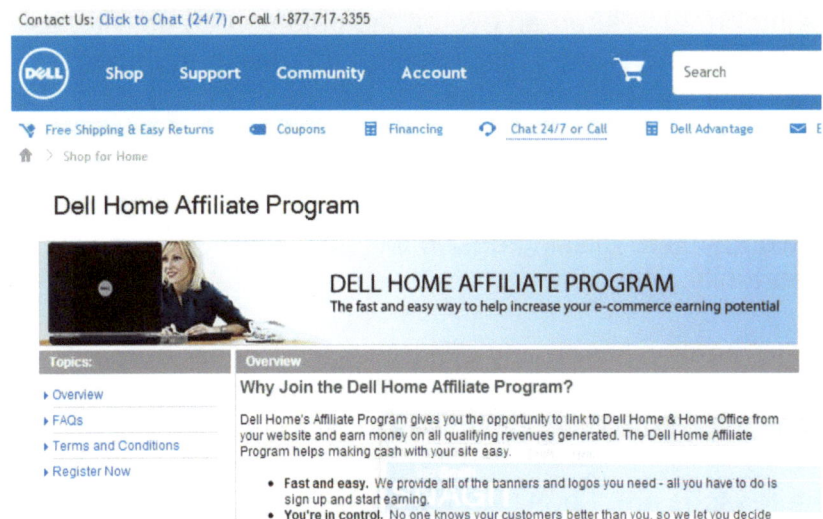

Most affiliate programs have one or two pages on their site about the affiliate program, but since you are reading this book, I know you want to be better than most affiliate programs.

In Part 3, which covers educating affiliates, I will go into depth on creating a resource site for your affiliates, which also has the added value of providing lots of relevant pages about your affiliate program for indexing by the search engines.

In addition to working on having your affiliate program show up high in the organic results, I suggest running a paid search campaign to recruit affiliates. Go slowly. Just bid on your company name and various combinations of the word affiliate. Keep an eye on how it's going and gradually add more generic terms to reach affiliates looking for your vertical, but not specifically your company.

Besides placing ads on the big search engines, test out Facebook Ads, too.

It's important to keep an eye on the paid search activity, as you can spend money fast if you're not paying attention.

Affiliate or CPA Network Site

Affiliates are looking for companies to promote within the networks, so if you've got an affiliate program that is not in a network, you're missing out on this passive recruiting opportunity.

Not to mention how many affiliates want to work only with affiliate programs in networks. With a small group of exceptions, I am one of them.

The reasons are: I don't want to have tons of logins; the networks can act as mediators if there is an issue; I like aggregated payments when I am testing new campaigns; and I have more trust in the network tracking over some home grown solution or a $100 software for tracking.

Also, I like the fact that I can compare data for a number of affiliate programs in the same niche, such as their EPC, cookie durations, and payout.

Another benefit of being in a network is that many of them offer enhanced placements to get more exposure for your affiliate program.

We run the [Affiliate Summit affiliate program on ShareASale](), and they offer a number of options to feature our affiliate program.

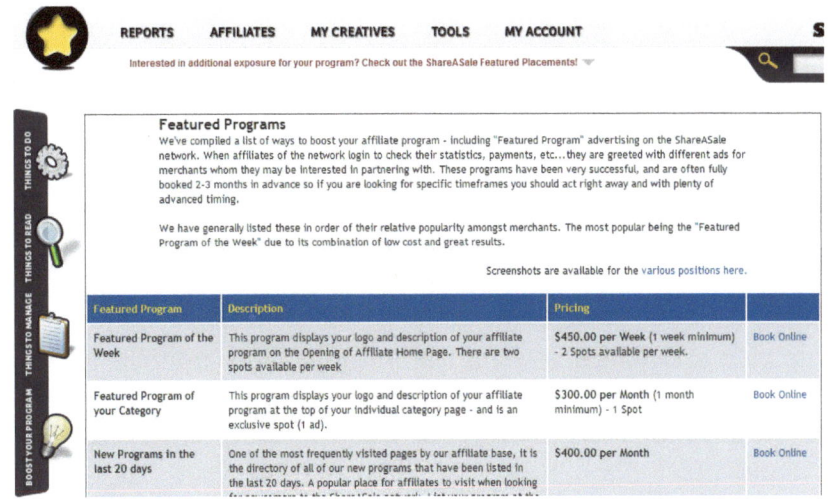

If you are not in a network currently, I strongly urge you to take a closer look at your network options. And, for those folks who are in networks, explore the paid options and revisit your description, categories, etc. to optimize your exposure.

I Check Out My Competitors' Websites

Every affiliate niche has leaders and influencers, and you can count on smaller affiliates copying the elements of the bigger affiliates, and not just the look and feel, but also the companies that they feature.

In essence, if you get placement with the big dogs, then you will get the benefit of the copycats expressing interest in your program, too.

Some big affiliates will sell premium placements for flat rates, enhanced commissions, or special privileges. So, in addition to the increased sales or leads you'll (hopefully) receive, those slots will help you recruit.

Word of Mouth

Just as affiliates are influenced by their competitors when it comes to which affiliate programs to promote, the word of mouth of their peers carries weight, as well.

And this can go both ways, as affiliates can become more or less interested in a given affiliate program, based on the positive or negative talk going around in chats, forums, social media, and other places.

This also should serve as a reminder to always strive to do right by affiliates. If something breaks with your affiliate program, fix it, and make good when affiliates are negatively impacted.

Affiliate Manager Website or Their Related Social Media Efforts

An affiliate manager website can take a number of forms, such as an Outsourced Program Manager (OPM) site, affiliate manager blog, or an affiliate resource site that is focused on an individual affiliate program.

The key is that affiliates like helpful affiliate managers because they know they will be able to count on them when there are problems.

Affiliate Summit polled affiliate marketers in 2012 to ask them which were the [best affiliate marketing blogs](). Check out that link to see examples.

Sharing advice, tips, news, and resources on a site is an effective way to help your current affiliates and to recruit new folks.

The same goes for social media. Having a presence on Facebook, Google+, LinkedIn, and Twitter is worth the effort. It enables you to promote affiliate programs and offers and to communicate with affiliates in the various places where they spend time.

While it can be a bit much to keep track of so many different social networks, HootSuite is a great tool for monitoring social media for mentions of your company and industry and for participating in the conversations.

I have a second monitor set up just to keep an eye on the various social networks and stay on top of what's being said.

I know it can be a little intimidating to establish a site if you haven't created one before. If this is where you are right now, you might want to check out my book, Extra Money Answer.

The book is focused on creating an affiliate site, but it also includes step-by-step instructions for setting up a domain and hosting for a WordPress blog.

Conferences

There are events for various affiliate and CPA networks throughout the year, as well as monthly affiliate marketing meetups, but the largest gatherings of affiliate marketers in the world are the Affiliate Summit conferences.

In full disclosure, in case you didn't read my bio in the book or we don't know each other already, I am a Co-Founder of Affiliate Summit.

I started Affiliate Summit with Missy Ward in 2003 for the purpose of providing educational sessions on the latest industry issues and fostering a productive networking environment for affiliate marketers.

We wanted to create a fun, vibrant, productive environment where the industry would join together to learn and do business.

There are two big events each year, and each one brings together thousands of affiliate marketers and hundreds of companies exhibiting across three days.

Attendees at Affiliate Summit events break out into five main categories: agencies, affiliates, merchants, networks, and vendors.

Affiliates account for about a third of attendees at Affiliate Summit.

Affiliate marketers fall into two categories, and they broke out at Affiliate Summit West 2013 as 60% concentrating on the sale of products or services vs. 40% focusing on lead generation.

The attendance at Affiliate Summit has grown steadily since the inception of the conferences in 2003.

One of the primary functions of the conferences is to bring together affiliates and merchants, and I certainly think it makes sense for affiliate managers to attend and meet up with current and future affiliates face to face.

There is a wide range of sponsor opportunities to fit all budgets, so affiliate managers running programs at any stage can have a presence and grow their businesses.

Contact Affiliate Summit with any questions about opportunities to meet and recruit affiliates at the conferences.

Print Publications

Last, but not least, on the list of places affiliates are finding affiliate programs, according to the 2013 Affiliate Summit AffStat Report, is print publications.

There are a number of business magazines that occasionally cover affiliate marketing, but FeedFront Magazine is focused specifically on the industry. In another bit of disclosure, I am the Co-Editor-in-Chief of FeedFront Magazine. This is a partnership with Missy Ward, too.

We started publishing the magazine in June 2008, and one of the reasons was we were frustrated with the inaccurate coverage of the industry. We sought to change that by creating a publication that was written entirely by the people in the trenches, instead of journalists.

That way the information is first hand and current. Also, the articles are a maximum of 500 words, so they get right to the point. No fluff.

FeedFront goes out to approximately 40,000 subscribers via USPS, and each issue is available to read online or download. So this is another way for an affiliate manager to get their program in front of affiliates.

I have a couple of other techniques I like to use to bring on quality affiliates…

Go after Your Customers

Ideally, your affiliates would be raving fans of your company, but it doesn't always work out that way. Plenty of affiliates are guns for hire. They will promote companies for the potential returns, and they really don't care about the brand or anything else.

But you have lots of people who are crazy about your products or services, and they are your regular customers. While many of these folks do not have a blog, email list, or other conventional affiliate method to get the word out for you, lots of them do have Facebook, Twitter, and other social media accounts.

Reach out to your customer base and sell them on the fun prospect of either earning cash or store credit. I buy things regularly on Amazon, so store credit is my preferred payment option as an affiliate there.

Your Payment Method

- **Pay me by Amazon.com gift certificate/card**
  ($10.00 minimum earnings)

  Your Amazon.com gift certificate/card will be sent to your primary email address

- **Pay me by direct deposit (United States Based Associates Only)**
  ($10.00 minimum earnings)
  (Direct Deposit is not available for international associates. Learn more)

- **Pay me by check**
  ($100.00 minimum earnings or choose your own threshold above the minimum.)

  Check processing fee applies - Learn More

If you have a customer email newsletter, that's a great place to regularly include information about your affiliate program.

Direct Mail

It might seem like taking a step backward to use direct mail to recruit new affiliates, but that mindset will keep you from one of the most impactful methods I've used to bring on quality affiliates and stay in touch with them.

I started using postcards back in 2000 to recruit affiliates for the ClubMom.com affiliate program.

The vendor I used back then would take a screen capture of a site and make that the front of the postcard. Then I got a few lines to write copy at the bottom.

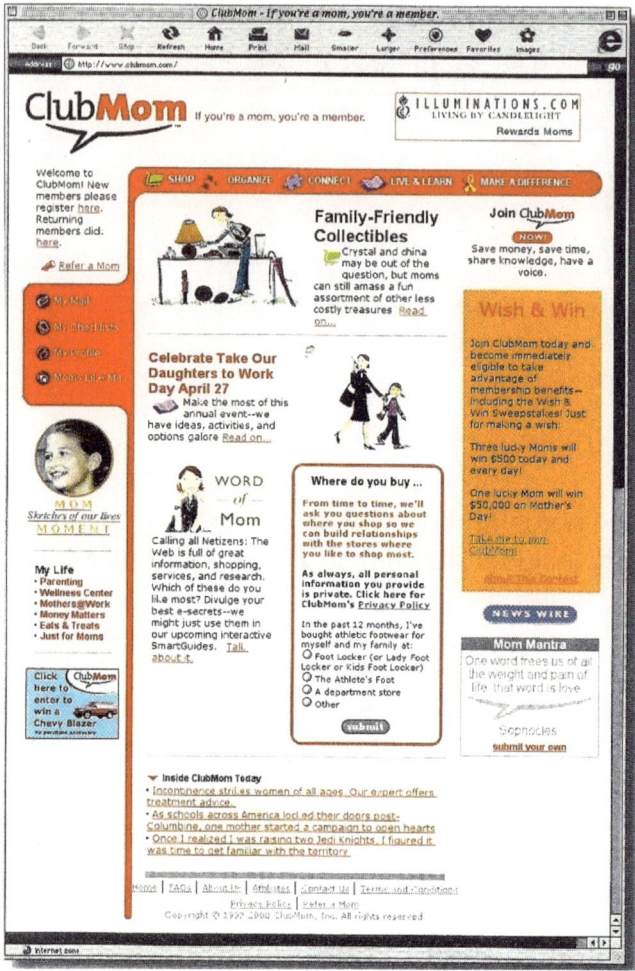

This solution was OK at the time, as I didn't know of other vendors that provided such a service, and I didn't have a graphic designer available to me.

That all changed over the years.

I was able to sell the affiliate program with the left side of the back of the postcard.

ClubMom
http://www.clubmom.com

ClubMom's Affiliate Program is:

- an easy way for you to earn cash by promoting the free ClubMom membership from your site
- an opportunity to add value to your Web site
- FREE

Affiliate Manager: Shawn Collins
Phone: 212-563-2223 x254
Fax: 212-563-2428
E-mail: scollins@clubmom-inc.com

After I was able to get access to a graphic designer, I mailed out a much more impactful postcard with the front focused solely on the affiliate program.

ClubMom Affiliate Program

Earn cash with your Web site or e-mail list.

- 365 day cookie
- Real-time stats
- Monthly checks
- Support 7 days a week

Apply now at clubmomaffiliates.com

This piece of mail was different from the previous one, as it had value propositions for the affiliate program on the front, and then I just put my contact information and how to apply on the back.

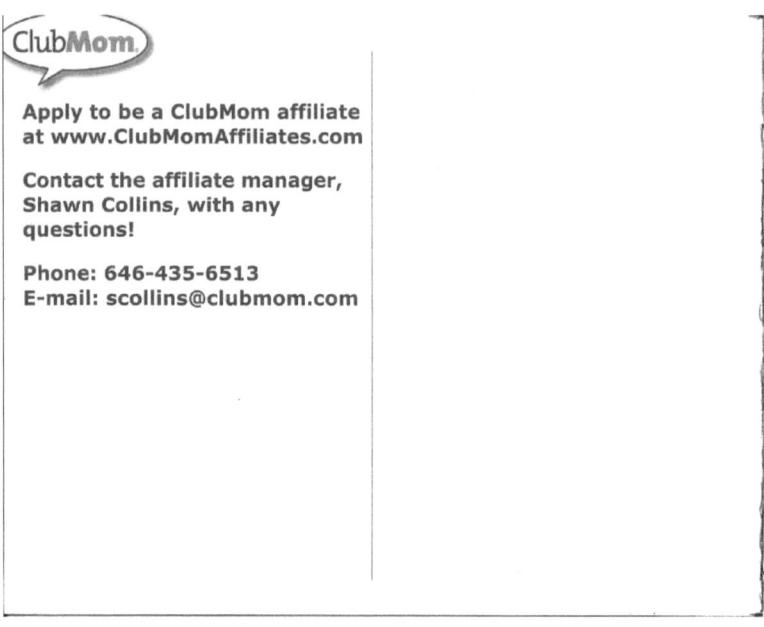

In 2003, I started managing additional affiliate programs on the side for the next few years. My first client was a cookie company called Chip 'N Dough, and I followed the postcard formula I used at ClubMom featuring value propositions of the affiliate program.

It worked, again. So I started using direct mail for all of my other clients. Here is a card I sent for Instrument Pro, a company that sells musical instruments.

As for finding the contact information of the affiliates I was targeting, I would first try their contact page. If that failed, I'd go to the WHOIS record for the owner of the domain.

While there are a variety of ways for an affiliate manager to contact affiliates directly, I found that direct mail was the most effective for me, based on surveying affiliates over the years about the reasons they applied to the affiliate program.

But still, I have gotten very few pieces of mail from affiliate programs over the years.

I highly recommend affiliate managers test direct mail to recruit affiliates. The fact that no one else is doing it is one of the best reasons for you to try – you'll really stick out.

PART 3

Educating Affiliates

"When you know better you do better." - Maya Angelou

So your affiliate recruitment efforts are starting to pay off. You've got quality affiliates on board and more are submitting applications to you on a daily basis.

You review each application and accept the affiliates that are top notch – the relevant, quality affiliates that want to promote your products and/or services.

But you're not done. You're never done with an affiliate program. Educating your affiliates should be an ongoing mission, so you can activate them and help optimize their efforts.

Resource Site

Let's start with a resource site for the affiliates. This is a stand-alone site that's dedicated to the affiliate program. I started creating these sites because I was frustrated with the process for updating the single page on the affiliate program at the company where I was working.

I would have to complete a form and send it to the IT department for things as simple as adding a link or fixing a typo. Then it could take days for them to get around to it.

Talk about frustrating.

So one day I petitioned my boss to let me create a site with the look and feel of the main company site, except that mine would consist of a handful of pages focused on the affiliate program. The domain would be the company name and the word "affiliates."

They went for it, and I created the site with a page for the affiliate program application, newsletter archive, affiliate agreement, a blog for updates and news, a contact form, FAQ, and a sales guide for the affiliates.

Back then, I created it by writing the HTML by hand, but you're lucky now that you can work it up in WordPress.

Frequently Asked Questions

I took a novel approach with the FAQ. I actually made it a place to see the answers to the "Frequently Asked Questions," since I was noticing that many affiliate programs would just put up a generic network FAQ.

My FAQ's had the information affiliates wanted to know right away, such as the policies on coupons, trademark bidding, email, and using the brand in a domain name, as well as suggested and prohibited keywords.

Sales Guide

And then there was the sales guide, which was my vision of a new employee guide for each affiliate program. My thought was that affiliates are partners and they should be given the tools they need to have the best chance at succeeding with the affiliate program.

Here is how I described the sales guide for Payless ShoeSource affiliates:

"Here at Payless ShoeSource, we consider our affiliate partners to be our sales team on the Web. And successful sales people take advantage of the tools and support at their disposal. We care about your success, and our main objective is for you to make lots of sales.

"This guide was designed to teach you how to promote the largest selection of Payless ShoeSource footwear anywhere. Payless ShoeSource sells one in every six pair of shoes sold in the United States, and we want to help you promote Payless ShoeSource's broad selection of quality, fashionable footwear in the most efficient and effective manner.

"We want every click to go to the most effective spot on our site, so that the traffic you generate for Payless ShoeSource converts into higher commissions for you. We know you can send us quality traffic and we want to pay you for it.

"Thank you for joining the Payless ShoeSource affiliate team and taking the time to read this sales guide. We look forward to building a strong and successful relationship with you."

In the case of Payless ShoeSource, the sales guide consisted of six sections, and I was regularly updating the information, based on comments and questions from the affiliates:

1. The Payless ShoeSource product and commission structure
2. Who is the Payless ShoeSource customer?
3. Eight things every Payless ShoeSource affiliate should know
4. Coupons for your customers
5. Additional tools to help you sell Payless ShoeSource
6. About Payless ShoeSource

Educate Yourself

Education is not just for your affiliates. In order to educate them, you need to be educated yourself.

If you are not an affiliate personally, have a look at my book, Extra Money Answer, to get some insight into creating an affiliate site.

It will enrich you to be an affiliate yourself, as you can better help your affiliates when you walk a mile in their shoes. Further, this will enable you to keep an eye on your competitors to monitor their creative, payout, etc. and constantly optimize your program.

Also, read FeedFront Magazine, which is free in the United States and published quarterly. Plus, we publish all of the past Affiliate Summit education sessions on video for free on YouTube. Watch and learn.

Bear in mind that different types of affiliates will need different types of advice on what they should be doing, so it's important for you to know about the challenges of content, coupon, data feed, email, mobile, paid search, rewards, social media, and video affiliates, so you can best serve them.

Share Information in Many Places

Some affiliates won't read all of your newsletters or visit your resource site, so make it a point to share your educational information on other platforms, too, where they might be more inclined to consume it.

I suggest setting up accounts for your affiliate program on SlideShare and YouTube. You also may want to consider a short podcast every week or so with the latest news on the affiliate program.

Yes, education for affiliates is an extra expense, in time and money, for your affiliate program. But what's the price of ignorance? Lower conversions, broken rules, unhappy affiliates.

Invest in the prosperity of your affiliates and you invest in your own success.

PART 4

Retaining Affiliates

"I hate losing more than I love winning." - Billy Beane (Moneyball)

Just because you manage to recruit an affiliate into your affiliate program doesn't mean they'll ever become active or even stick around.

Retention is vital, and the failure to recognize that can be fatal to an affiliate program.

Conferences and Tradeshows

Face-to-face interaction is important in a business relationship, and conferences and tradeshows facilitate these meetings in a variety of ways.

For instance, many companies will host dinners, happy hours, or other get-togethers to meet with their affiliates during [Affiliate Summit](). The event runs for three full days, and many people are in the city where it takes place for 4-5 days.

Additionally, there are sponsorship opportunities to get tables or booths, and there are other ways to have a presence at the conference.

These enable an affiliate program or outsourced program management (OPM) company to have a "home base" at the conference so their affiliates can easily find them.

Whether there is a dedicated exhibitor space or not, the important thing is to be there in person when your affiliates are there for some quality time in person.

Make It Easy to Contact You

It's tough to maintain relationships with your affiliates if they are not able to easily reach out to you.

Provide your direct email address and phone number, as well as other methods to reach you, such as IM/Skype, Twitter, and Facebook.

And be sure to let them know your name. It's very off-putting for affiliates to get emails signed generically by the Affiliate Manager with no real name attached.

Sharing Information and News

You should send communications to your affiliates on a regular basis, not only to remind them that you are there to assist them, but also to keep them up to date on the latest creative, promotions, etc.

Send out an email newsletter monthly, but don't limit your mass communications to email only. You should provide your information in all of the places where affiliates want to consume it, such as an affiliate blog, newsletter, Twitter, Facebook, and video.

In the [2013 Affiliate Summit AffStat Report](), affiliates were asked "What is your preferred method for finding out information from an affiliate manager?"

Here is how affiliate preferences for communications broke out.

 11.4%
BLOG OR COMPANY WEBSITE

 17.1%
MASS EMAIL FROM THE AFFILIATE MANAGER

 56.3%
EMAIL FROM AN AFFILIATE NETWORK

 1.9%
TWITTER

 1.3%
FACEBOOK

 1.3%
VIDEO

OTHER 10.8%

One way to build efficiency into this process, especially if you can get affiliates to opt-in to a list outside of your affiliate network, is to have your blog content syndicated to email, Twitter, and Facebook.

I use AWeber to push my blog RSS feed to email and then HootSuite to syndicate that content to Twitter, Facebook, and other social media sites.

Direct Mail

In Part 2 on recruiting affiliates, I mentioned using direct mail as a method to recruit affiliates, but it also can be used as a retention method.

Here is a postcard I sent to existing affiliates in late December 2003.

There was a bit of an evolution here, besides, as the back of this postcard included my AIM at the time (note – this was before the ninja thing was all played out) and my home phone number to reach me outside of office hours.

The ClubMom family wishes you a very happy holiday season. We look forward to working with you in 2004 and beyond.

Login to your account at www.ClubMomAffiliates.com

Contact your affiliate manager, Shawn Collins, 7 days a week:

- scollins@clubmom.com
- AOL IM: affiliateninja
- Weekdays: 646-435-6513
- Weekends: 908-522-0056

Affiliates regularly remarked how they loved that I made myself available whenever they needed me, but the reality was that I didn't hear from them too often outside of the office.

When I did, I was happy to help, because I knew most other affiliate managers wouldn't do that when they were "off the clock."

Custom Creative

While you should have all of the typical sizes for banner creative already, there are some affiliates who will have special needs for the unique dimensions of their sites or newsletters.

In some cases, they will do it themselves, but you don't want that happening, because they might not represent your brand the way you want them to with the quality of the creative and/or the copy on it.

Put it out there that you are willing to provide custom creative for any affiliates that request it. Those who have these needs will really appreciate it.

Promotions and Incentives

The affiliates who can move the needle for you will expect higher commission rates than you offer publicly. The listed commission rate is considered a base rate by many affiliates.

Look into providing both an immediate raise to some affiliates and increased commission based on volume for others.

You also should run contests to get affiliates to increase their promotional efforts for you and compete with each other. Provide bonuses for the biggest performers.

But you don't want to alienate the majority of affiliates who never will be in the top 5% or so. The solution is to put on contests to encourage various actions, such as increasing exposure, generating more sales, showing the biggest improvement month over month, and simply becoming active.

TL;DR

That stands for "too long; didn't read," in case you didn't know.

For anyone who skipped to here from the beginning in order to get a summary of everything in a few sentences... Come on!

Why did you even buy this if you weren't going to read it?

The subtitle really says it all. As an affiliate manager, it's not enough to just recruit affiliates. You need an ongoing program of recruiting, educating, and retaining affiliates.

But still, I'd urge you to go back and read what I have to say about each area. I kept this nice and short so you could blast through it in one sitting. Take some time and read it. I think it will be worth your while.

Good luck with your affiliate program(s)!

Resources for Affiliate Managers

There are lots of low cost and free tools and resources out there for affiliate managers. Here are some that I would recommend:

- Affiliate Program Management: An Hour a Day by Geno Prussakov
- FeedFront Magazine – free quarterly subscription in the U.S.
- GeekCast – marketing podcasts
- Affiliate Summit videos – videos of past educational sessions
- AffStat – annual benchmarking report on the affiliate marketing industry
- Affiliate marketing blogs – top blogs in affiliate marketing

I also have a frequently updated list of general business and marketing resources online. Check out my resources for affiliate marketers.

www.ingramcontent.com/pod-product-compliance
Lightning Source LLC
Chambersburg PA
CBHW040931180526
45159CB00002BA/691